# AMSTERDA
## THE CITY AT A GLA

 **Anne Frank House**
This iconic museum is a
within the city centre.
*See p013*

**Bloemenmarkt**
Browse through the stalls selling bulbs
and plants of every description.
*Singel*

**Centraal Station**
The 19th-century station is the city's
main transport hub.
*Stationsplein*

**Van Gogh Museum**
The artist's work is on show in the main
museum, while Kisho Kurokawa's wing
houses temporary exhibitions.
*See p014*

**Rijksmuseum**
Dating from 1885, this museum houses
the nation's Golden Age treasures.
*Stadhouderskade 42, T 674 7047*

**NEMO**
Renzo Piano's ship-like science museum
raises the skyline of the otherwise flat
Sporenburg Peninsula.
*See p012*

**KNSM Island**
Escape the canals and witness the ongoing
evolution of this former cargo dock.
*Borneo Sporenburg*

# INTRODUCTION
## THE CHANGING FACE OF THE URBAN SCENE

Like Venice, Amsterdam is a grand, architectural marvel set within a warren of ancient canals that has survived the shifting, silty sands of time. But, unlike its Italian counterpart, it remains a vibrant, evolving metropolis and not a bejewelled empty husk of a museum piece. A glimpse into the uncurtained, stately windows of many of the canal houses that line its four principal waterways speaks volumes about the city's psyche. Often modernised and always welcoming, these 17th-century spaces reveal an artistic, mercantile people with an irreverent, quirky sense of humour, which is evident in the work of the creative mavens who took the global design stage by storm at the start of the new millennium.

Ever wily to the winds of change, Amsterdam has picked up on the success of designers Marcel Wanders, Hella Jongerius and the progeny of Droog by producing a string of new hotels, restaurants, bars and clubs to meet the modern needs of its many visitors. And to accommodate the swelling number of Amsterdammers, a brave new world of futuristic developments has emerged from reclaimed land in Havens Oost, the eastern docklands.

In these times of climate change, the city may eventually lose its battle with the sea, though if that little Dutch boy of legend takes his proverbial finger out of the dyke, the tourists will still come in their thousands, perhaps by submarine. And then perhaps this city will become the Atlantis of our time.

# ESSENTIAL INFO
## FACTS, FIGURES AND USEFUL ADDRESSES

**TOURIST OFFICE**
*Centraal Station*
*Stationsplein 2b*
*T 551 2525*
*www.amsterdamtourist.nl*

**TRANSPORT**
**Bicycle rental**
MacBike, *T 620 0985*
*www.macbike.nl*
**Car hire**
Avis, *T 683 6061*
Hertz, *T 612 2441*
**Taxis**
Taxicentral, *T 677 7777*
Watertaxi, *T 535 6363*

**EMERGENCY SERVICES**
**Central Medical Service**
*T 592 3434*
**Emergencies**
*112*
**Police (non-emergencies)**
*T 0900 8844*
**24-hour pharmacy**
Pharmacy Kruidvat
*Loofvald 40*
*T 647 3489*

**CONSULATES**
**British Consulate**
*Koningslaan 44*
*T 676 4343*
**US Consulate**
*Museumplein 19*
*T 575 5309*

**MONEY**
**American Express**
*Damrak 66*
*T 504 8770*
*www10.americanexpress.com*

**POSTAL SERVICES**
**Post Office**
Hoofdpostkantoor PTT
*Singel 250*
**Shipping**
UPS
*T 0800 099 1300*
*www.ups.com*

**BOOKS**
**Amsterdam: A Literary Companion**
edited by Mandfred Wolf
(Whereabouts Press)
**Anne Frank Remembered** by Miep Gies
(Simon & Schuster)
**Planning Amsterdam** by Allard Jolles
and Erik Klusman (Netherlands
Architectural Institute)

**WEBSITES**
**Art**
*www.rijksmuseum.nl*
*www.stedelijk.nl*
*www.vangoghmuseum.nl*
**Design**
*www.westergasfabriek.com*
**Newspapers**
*www.nrc.nl*
*www.telegraaf.nl*

**COST OF LIVING**
**Taxi from airport**
**to city centre**
€39
**Cappuccino**
€2.20
**Packet of cigarettes**
€4.60
**Daily newspaper**
€1.10
**Bottle of champagne**
€75

**AMSTERDAM**
**Area**
114 sq km
**Population**
735,000
**Currency**
Euro €1 = £0.70 = $1.20
**Telephone codes**
The Netherlands: 31
Amsterdam: 20
**Time**
GMT +1

NETHERLANDS

London

Amsterdam

Paris

**AVERAGE MAX TEMPERATURE / °C**

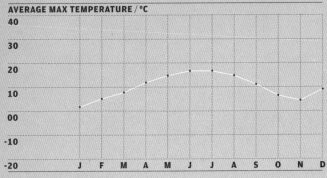

| 40 | | | | | | | | | | | | |
| 30 | | | | | | | | | | | | |
| 20 | | | | | | | | | | | | |
| 10 | | | | | | | | | | | | |
| 00 | | | | | | | | | | | | |
| -10 | | | | | | | | | | | | |
| -20 | J | F | M | A | M | J | J | A | S | O | N | D |

**AVERAGE RAINFALL / MM**

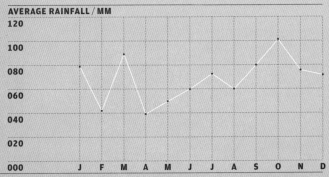

| 120 | | | | | | | | | | | | |
| 100 | | | | | | | | | | | | |
| 080 | | | | | | | | | | | | |
| 060 | | | | | | | | | | | | |
| 040 | | | | | | | | | | | | |
| 020 | | | | | | | | | | | | |
| 000 | J | F | M | A | M | J | J | A | S | O | N | D |

# NEIGHBOURHOODS
## THE AREAS YOU NEED TO KNOW AND WHY

To help you navigate the city, we've chosen the most interesting districts (see the map inside the back cover) and underlined featured venues in colour, according to their location (see below); those venues that are outside these areas are not coloured.

### DE PIJP

This small district to the south of the city centre claims to be the most multicultural in Europe. Ever since its studenty and artistic residents were joined by the expats and media types wanting to buy into bohemian Amsterdam, the area has become extremely trendy. De Pijp's daily Albert Cuyp market is a local institution definitely worth a visit, but you should also head south to admire the enclave around Henriette Ronnerplein, which was built by the Amsterdam School architectural movement.

### WESTERPARK

The recent conversion of a 19th-century gas works, the Westergasfabriek, into an arts complex surrounded by parkland has revived the fortunes of this area. This year, a cinema opens to complement the existing gallery and bar, with theatres and restaurants following in 2007. The area around Haarlemmerstraat is fast evolving into a hot new neighbourhood full of boutiques, delis and trendy restaurants.

### CENTRUM

Amsterdam's notorious red-light district is located in the heart of the city, and is ringed by the four 17th-century canals: Prinsengracht, Keizersgracht, Herengracht and Singel. The area is crowned by the stately Centraal Station, the city's impressive neo-Renaissance gateway to the rest of Holland and Europe.

### JORDAAN

When the city's aristocracy constructed their elegant canal houses in the 17th century, they also built the Jordaan, to house craftsmen, brewers, tanners and merchants, and to keep them on the other side of Prinsengracht. For centuries, Jordaaners formed a tightly knit community, but the area's charming streets are now the stomping ground of the thirtysomethings who frequent its bars and restaurants.

### HAVENS OOST

The man-made islands of KNSM, Java and Borneo Sporenburg began life as humble wave-breaks and the home of the warehouses and offices of local shipping companies. Today, state-of-the-art housing and innovative architecture have attracted hordes of young families, and the area has become decidedly desirable.

### OUD ZUID

The end of the 19th century saw Amsterdam expand beyond the watery borders of Nassaukade, Mauritskade and Stadhouderskade. Oud Zuid became one of the most important new districts in this evolution. The large, landscaped green space of Vondelpark prompted the construction of many a mansion to overlook the park, while the cultural playground that is Museumplein, just south of Leidseplein, has always attracted art lovers in their droves.

# LANDMARKS

## THE SHAPE OF THE CITY SKYLINE

Amsterdam is a place that you visit, and while visiting long to live in, because it has everything that you could ever want from a city. A compact place, it is just right for aimless strolling and, above all, it offers a simple civic lesson: raise tolerance to the level of principle and there will, after a time, be little need to exercise it.

As with most northern European cities, Amsterdam is predicated on the need and the desire to be tucked up at home for a good chunk of the year. At the same time, here the indoors is always on display for all to see. In Amsterdam, the temptation is to go not window shopping, but window living. What must it be like to live in one of those high-ceilinged apartments on Prinsengracht, with their exquisite lights and minimal decor? Or to gaze out at the canals, which, here and there, reflect the lights hung under the bridges to form magical, sparkling yellow necklaces. All of which is to say that Amsterdam's charms are discreet ones.

This is one of the world's great walking cities, but, unlike in New York or Paris, the way here is seldom marked by the narcissistic tower block or the dominating civic structure. For a chance to relieve your eyes from the gorgeous claustrophobia of the canals, head out to KNSM Island, the squeaky clean eastern dockside development that takes the concept of an Amsterdam vernacular and blows it out of the water.

*For all addresses, see Resources.*

## The Whale

Even among the multitude of modern buildings that comprise the Sporenburg Peninsula redevelopment project, this housing complex stands out. The size of a football stadium, and suitably grey in colour, it squats in the former harbour just like a beached whale, hence its name. Completed in 2000 by architects Cie, and one of only three large-scale buildings in an area where low rise predominates, the Whale is an incredibly sophisticated mixed-use, though mostly residential, development. The roof is angled to elevate the building on two sides and maximise sunlight in the apartments within. Although these are off limits to all but the most charming of visitors, there are regular openings and fashion events held in the complex, so it's worth checking what's on before you visit.
*Baron GA Tindalplein, Borneo Sporenburg, www.cie.nl*

## NEMO

The roof of Renzo Piano's ship-like science museum is conceived as a city square, the modern equivalent of the elegant spaces back in the historic centre. It's just about the only raised public area in this famously flat city and draws considerable summer crowds. It offers a good view back to old Amsterdam, although the building, surrounded by water on three sides, is closer in spirit to the massive Borneo Sporenburg dockland area, where much of the city's boldest architecture is concentrated. When it opened, in 1997, it was dismissed by local architects as 'half a Renzo Piano' building because they felt corners had been cut on the finish and choice of materials in order to hit a notoriously tight budget. Gradually, though, it's become a firm local favourite.
*Oosterdok 2, T 531 3233, www.e-nemo.nl*

### Anne Frank House

If countless school trips put you off yet another visit to the wonderful Anne Frank House, the building, and particularly its 1999 extension by architects Benthem Crouwel, should be reason enough to tempt you back. It's also a useful landmark within the city centre, especially when it is lit up at night. And to make your visit worthwhile, the nearby area of Jordaan is to neighbourhoods what Amsterdam is to cities – small but perfectly formed. Jordaan has so much: cafés, markets, studios and slick galleries. It even has a strong residue of authentic blue-collar life, which appeals to the hipsters and professionals who have moved in to live out a utopian vision of what the Dutch mercifully don't call *la vie bohème*. *Prinsengracht 267, T 556 7105, www.annefrank.org*

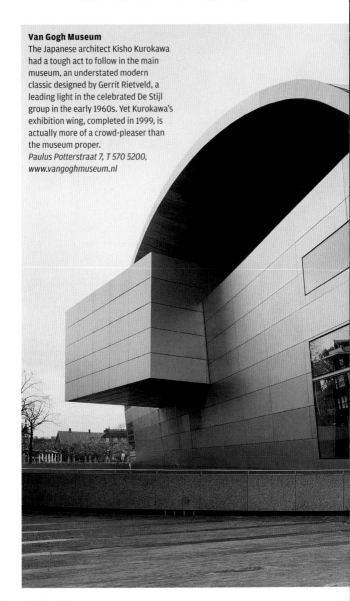

### Van Gogh Museum

The Japanese architect Kisho Kurokawa had a tough act to follow in the main museum, an understated modern classic designed by Gerrit Rietveld, a leading light in the celebrated De Stijl group in the early 1960s. Yet Kurokawa's exhibition wing, completed in 1999, is actually more of a crowd-pleaser than the museum proper.
*Paulus Potterstraat 7, T 570 5200, www.vangoghmuseum.nl*

# HOTELS

## WHERE TO STAY AND WHICH ROOMS TO BOOK

Like Paris and Barcelona, Amsterdam is a classic mini-break destination. Its tiny size and limited capacity mean the city's hotels are often booked up in advance, especially from March, when the tulips first appear, until mid September. In the 1980s and 1990s, the range of accommodation was restricted to grotty flophouses for stoner students, the odd gem, such as the Canal House Hotel (Keizersgracht 148, T 622 5182), mid-range corporate monoliths, and three grandes dames – The Grand (Oudezijds Voorburgwal 197, T 555 3111), Amsterdam American (Leidsekade 97, T 556 3000) and the Amstel (see p024). Then the Dutch design revolution at the dawn of the new millennium put paid to all that.

Hotel Seven One Seven (see p020), The College Hotel (see p018) and The Dylan (see p028) all have a refined, classic style; Lute Suites (see p021), Lloyd Hotel, Hotel Arena (see p030) and Hotel V (Victorieplein 42, T 662 3233) attract a design-savvy crowd on wide-ranging budgets, while Amsterdam's b&bs are modernising fast. If 't Hotel (see p025) is full, try Kien (Tweede Weteringdwarsstraat 65, T 428 5262) or Marcel's Creative Exchange (Leidsestraat 87, T 622 9834). Once an acclaimed graphic designer, Marcel van Woerkom opened up his 17th-century townhouse as an artists' retreat 35 years ago. The four rooms hung with original artwork now have a cool retro feel, particularly the Style Room. *For all addresses and room rates, see Resources.*

### Lloyd Hotel

Although the Lloyd, which is located in the trendy eastern docklands area, has been given a new lease of life by the big stars of Dutch design (Claudy Jongstra, Hella Jongerius and Marcel Wanders), it can't be defined as just another fancy design hotel. Guests can choose from five room categories, which range from functional one-star pods with shared bathrooms to five-star suites – one has a grand piano, another boasts a free-standing fibreglass bath, while the most popular features a 4m-wide bed that sleeps eight. The hotel's restaurant, Snel, is equally innovative, as dishes can be eaten in any order, sent up to your room or taken away.
*Oosterlijke Handelskade 34, T 561 3636, www.lloydhotel.com*

## The College Hotel

This recent addition to Amsterdam's hotel scene, located minutes from Vondelpark and Museumplein, takes its name from the listed 1894 college building in which it is housed. Classrooms have been tastefully converted into 40 luxurious rooms with a contemporary yet classic style. What was the gym is now a restaurant serving à la carte breakfasts, traditional Dutch dishes for lunch, and an innovative take on the local cuisine for dinner. The lounge bar has several intimate seating areas and the poshest loos in town. The service can be patchy, as many of the staff are students from a local hotel school, though at least the scholastic theme is being continued. *Roelof Hartstraat 1, T 571 1511, www.thecollegehotel.com*

## Hotel Seven One Seven

With eight huge suites, an eclectic decor that mixes antiques with modern pieces, and a canalside location in a handsome 18th-century canal house, Seven One Seven is the most elegant guesthouse in town. Real fires in winter, leafy, lovingly tended courtyards in summer, breakfast hampers delivered to your room, and an atmosphere of refined discretion make this an intimate retreat, and the perfect pad for a romantic liaison. Booking well in advance is essential, as the hotel is a favourite among CEOs and visiting dignitaries. Try to reserve the Picasso Suite, or the particularly private Schubert Suite (above), which has beamed ceilings and Franco-Dutch interiors.
*Prinsengracht 717, T 427 0717, www.717hotel.nl*

### Lute Suites

Design meets gastronomy at this former 17th-century gunpowder factory, which has been converted into seven apartments by chef Peter Lute and design supremo Marcel Wanders. The interiors could best be described as modern baroque, while design junkies can enjoy various Wanders prototypes, as well as his quirky set pieces. Suite Five (above) is the most striking, and features a mezzanine wet room dominated by the egg-shaped 'Soap' bath that Wanders designed for Boffi. Suite Seven sports the designer's iconic 'Knotted' chair, made of rope soaked in glue. Each of the suites has a kitchenette, although guests are unlikely to tire of the hotel's excellent restaurant, which has a menu that changes daily. *Amsteldijk Zuid 54-58, Ouderkerk aan den Amstel, T 472 2462, www.lutesuites.com*

### InterContinental Amstel

Since it opened in 1867, the Amstel has prided itself as the being the most luxurious hotel in the city, although these days its opulent interiors make it feel a little dated. Yet the marble staircase in the lobby (above), the multilingual staff, the sharp service and the Michelin-starred restaurant, La Rive, put the Amstel in a different league to your average InterConti. The hotel's sublime location, overlooking the Amstel, and its palatial proportions, make it an impressive destination, and the hotel of choice for visiting royalty. The place was packed out for Prince Willem Alexander's wedding a few years ago. *Professor Tulpplein 1, T 622 6060, www.ichotelsgroup.com*

#### 't Hotel

Hidden behind a typical Amsterdam curiosity shop, selling art deco lamps and ceramics, books on Bauhaus architecture and, weirdly, a selection of ladies' hats, 't Hotel is one of the city's best b&bs. Three of the eight rooms overlook the impossibly romantic Leliegracht, which runs perpendicular to the main canals of Keizersgracht and Herengracht. Room 8 (pictured overleaf) on the top floor is a huge loft space that sleeps up to five. It has glorious views of the immaculate courtyard gardens next door, though you should be prepared to lug your bags up the steep, rickety staircase, as the hotel has no lift. The lack of an in-house restaurant is more than made up for by the owners' encyclopedic knowledge of all the great restaurants and bars in the area. *Leliegracht 18, T 422 2741, www.thotel.nl*

### The Dylan

Under new management, the hotel formerly known as Blakes has lost its original name, but not its exquisite interiors, which are still subject to the obsessive eye of the hotel's creator and interior designer, Anouska Hempel. The slick, white, orchid-bedecked rooms hark back to the minimalist style of her eponymous former property in London, although guests at The Dylan have the choice of cosier rooms, furnished with reams of fabric and stacks of colour-coordinated cushions. The hotel's inviting lounge/bar area, restaurant and courtyard (right) are usually liberally sprinkled with the black-polo-neck-and-designer-shades brigade, which gives the place an air of glamorous intrigue. The Dylan would be an ideal setting for a latter-day Agatha Christie thriller.

*Keizersgracht 384, T 530 2010,*
*www.dylanamsterdam.com*

## Hotel Arena

After a multimillion-euro makeover at the beginning of the new millennium, Arena is no longer the lowly backpack-shack full of stoned teenagers that it was in the 1980s. Today, it attracts a slightly older, more sophisticated clientele. Contemporary interiors and furnishings by Piet Hein Eek, Ineke Hans and Marcel Wanders complement the original features of this large complex, originally built in 1890 as an orphanage. The hotel's restaurant (left), designed by local creative legend Ronald Hoofd, has a fine terrace, while the nightclub, which is housed in the former chapel, is an Amsterdam institution. Grooving in the nave when Hed Kandi DJs take to the decks is an experience not to be missed. *'s-Gravesandestraat 51, T 694 7444, www.hotelarena.nl*

# 24 HOURS

## SEE THE BEST OF THE CITY IN JUST ONE DAY

For such a small city, Amsterdam packs a mean cultural punch. The Dutch Golden Age painters and the mad, maverick post-Impressionist Van Gogh still top the charts at the world's most prestigious auction houses, and many of their most famous works hang in the city's museums. Scaffolding currently covers much of the Rijksmuseum (Stadhouderskade 42, T 674 7000), but highlights from its permanent collection can be seen at 'The Masterpieces' exhibition, and a satellite show is on view at Schiphol airport. In 2006, Rembrandt House (Jodenbreestraat 4, T 520 0400) spearheaded national celebrations of the 400th anniversary of the artist's birth, while Anne Frank House (see p013) is testament to the city's darkest hour. The Stedelijk Museum and FOAM Photography Museum (Keizersgracht 609, T 551 6500) are powerful platforms for modern and contemporary forms of expression, and even the Nieuwe Kerk (Dam Square, T 638 6909), the stately venue for royal ceremonies, puts on world-class exhibitions.

No trip to Amsterdam would be complete without a tour of the 17th-century canals at its core, which can be explored by bike (www.macbike.nl), from the water (www.canal.nl), or even by motorised scooter (www.segwayguidedtours.com). And for those who want to experience the very soul of the city, a Like-a-Local tour (www.like-a-local.com) provides a real Amsterdammer as a guide. *For all addresses, see Resources.*

### 09.00 Stedelijk Museum

Start the day with the legendary full Irish breakfast at Barney's (T 625 9761) on trendy Haarlemmerstraat. Then make your way past the magnificent, neo-Renaissance Centraal Station to Amsterdam's contemporary art museum, the Stedelijk, housed temporarily in the old Post Office building. After taking in an exhibition, peruse the postcards and art books in the well-stocked shop, then head upstairs to 11 (above; T 625 5999). Over a *koffie verkeert* (that's a Dutch caffè latte) and a slice of *appeltaart* (apple tart) sprinkled with cinnamon, enjoy the best views in the city, and even more art. *Oosterdokskade 5, T 573 2911, www.stedelijk.nl*

### 11.00 Amstelkring Museum

Walk down to Oudezijds Voorburgwal, a quay once known as 'Velvet Canal', because of the obscene wealth of its burghers. Residents are better known today for their obscene acts, as this is the heart of the red-light district. Step back into the 17th century at the Amstelkring Museum, where the original interiors have been preserved downstairs; upstairs you will find the second most famous loft in Amsterdam, after Anne Frank's. This secret chapel (above), Our Lord in the Attic, was built in 1663 as a response to the anti-papal stance of the infant Dutch Republic, which forced Catholic kitsch behind closed doors. Afterwards, stop to admire the Oude Kerk, which is located just a block away.

*Oudezijds Voorburgwal 40, T 624 6604, www.museumamstelkring.nl*

### 12.30 Amsterdam Historical Museum

Continue down the same quay, taking a right down Damstraat to Dam Square, which is presided over by the Koninklijk Paleis (town hall), then head south to Amsterdam's Historical Museum. Wander through the Civil Guard's gallery (above), the only gallery in the world where paintings are displayed on a covered public street, and admire the severe but elegant portraits of the city's 17th-century militia. If you have time, take a turn round the Begijnhof, the most famous and picturesque of Amsterdam's almshouse courtyards, then enjoy a canalside lunch at Walem (T 625 3544) or Morlangs (T 625 2681) next door.
*Kalverstraat 92, T 523 1822,*
*www.ahm.nl*

### 15.00 Van Gogh Museum

Head south to the Van Gogh Museum, the highlight of the cultural grand prix that is Museumplein. The audio tour offers an excellent introduction to his one prolific decade of painting, when he produced 800 canvases, a quarter of which are displayed in this building. Works by Van Gogh's contemporaries – Gauguin, Monet, Toulouse-Lautrec – put his work into context, but pale beside his depiction of bleak poverty in the *Potato Eaters*, the dark and sinister *Cornfield with Crows*, and joyous celebration of new life depicted in *Almond Blossom*, which Van Gogh painted to celebrate the birth of his nephew. If visiting on a Friday, avoid the daytime crowds and schedule an evening tour (the museum is open until 10pm). *Paulus Potterstraat 7, T 570 5200, www.vangoghmuseum.nl*

### 19.30 Dinner

To sample Dutch cuisine, make your way
to The College Hotel (see p018), for
cocktails in the lounge and a meal in the
restaurant. Experiencing the cutting-edge,
multicultural district of nearby De Pijp is
another alternative – eat and drink until
the early hours at 18twintig (T 470 0651).
If you have the energy for another leg in
your cultural marathon, make sure you
book tickets for an evening tour (until
8.30pm; tickets available from the tourist
office on Leidseplein) at Anne Frank House
(T 556 7100). Follow your tour with early
evening drinks at Werck (T 627 4079),
located opposite (the roof terrace is
fantastic in summer), then dinner at
The Dylan (see p028; right), where head
chef Dennis Kuipers (formerly of the
Amstel; see p024) fuses modern French
and North African cuisine.
*Keizersgracht 384, T 530 2010,*
*www.dylanamsterdam.com*

# URBAN LIFE
## CAFÉS, RESTAURANTS, BARS AND NIGHTCLUBS

Drinking and eating out in Amsterdam is a seasonal affair. When the bulbs have finished blooming in May, the *nieuwe haring* (new herring) season begins and locals indulge in the Dutch answer to sashimi, which they garnish with chopped onion and gherkin and buy from street stalls – the best are on Koningsplein and at the beginning of Singel near Centraal Station. The streets that line the canals become a continental café scene between midday and midnight, when open sandwiches washed down with a *witbier* with a slice of lemon become the order of the day. When the sun is out, enjoy an alfresco lunch at Lunchcafé Singel 404 (Singel 404, T 428 0154), Walem (Keizersgracht 449, T 625 3544) or Morlangs (451 Keizersgracht 449, T 625 2681). If you're near Bloemenmarkt, head for Café De Jaren (Nieuwe Doelenstraat 20-22, T 625 5771), and before or after a visit to Museumplein stroll through Vondel-park, stopping at Het Blauwe Theehuis (T 662 0254).

In summer, DJs strike up lounge sets on decked terraces, no-tably at Onassis (see p044) and Odessa (Veemkade 259, T 419 3010), a Ukrainian trade ship converted into a retro restaurant and bar in the old port east of Centraal Station. In winter, classic, warming dishes, such as pea soup or game, will help dispel the biting cold. Make a reservation at D'Vijff Vlieghen (Spuistraat 294-302, T 530 4060) or at The College Hotel (see p018) restaurant. *For all addresses, see Resources.*

## Supperclub

Love it or hate it, Supperclub launched the city's lounge culture. Around a decade ago, architectural practice Concrete gave an abandoned church a futuristic facelift and created a club that has since become an international brand. A cross between a Friday night and a Sunday morning, Supperclub serves film producers, starlets and mafiosi lying prostrate on extra-wide white banquettes. The waiting staff are gorgeous and the DJs play the latest lounge and club tracks set to psychedelic visuals, interspersed with lip-synching drag acts, crooning cabaret singers and performance artists best described as experimental.
*Jonge Roelensteeg 21, T 344 6400, www.supperclub.nl*

La Chambre Obscure, Supperclub

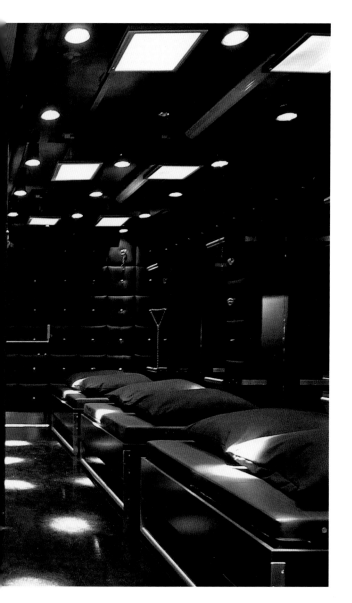

### Onassis

In 2005, four of Amsterdam's movers and shakers got together to transform a former shipping factory west of Centraal Station into a sleek lounge/restaurant called Onassis. The space was designed by local architects Dedato and mimics a sleek, luxurious ship. Guests can cosy up in leather booths and perch on bar stools inside, or venture outside to lie on pillows on the expansive 400-sq m deck.

The simple but sophisticated Italian menu of pasta and grilled fish dishes was created by Carmine D'Antuono, who owns the stylish restaurant Cinema Paradiso. The live music and DJ sets at Onassis are arranged by Rob Benoni, the owner of the brown café Finch (T 626 2461).
*Westerdoksdijk 40, T 330 0456, www.onassisamsterdam.nl*

### Envy

Another eaterie from the owners of Supperclub, Envy has been stampeded by local fashionistas and foodies since it opened in 2005. Concrete designed a long, open kitchen by the entrance, which is lit by large Tom Dixon mirror-ball lights and lined with fridges that showcase wines, cheeses and sausages flown in daily from Italy. The dining area is a moody, black space (Envy is open for dinner only), illuminated to flatter both the sophisticated clientele and excellent antipasti on offer. Highlights from the menu include Serrano ham with truffle foam, and green asparagus with goat's cheese fondue.

*Prinsengracht 381, T 344 6407, www.envy.nl*

### Brasserie Harkema

When Amsterdam's legendary nightclub
Roxy burned down in 1999, the owner,
Michiel Kleiss, turned his talent to
catering, and in 2003 opened the huge
bar/bodega/brasserie Harkema.
Architects Herman Prast and Ronald
Hooft converted this former tobacco
factory in the heart of town into an
industrial, split-level space, setting
a spectacular window into its facade.

The bar and main dining area are
separated by an opaque metal curtain.
The open kitchen boasts a vast wine rack
and turns out affordable, well-executed
dishes. Brasserie Harkema's central
location tucked down a tiny slip road
has made it a hit with Amsterdammers
and visitors alike.
*Nes 67, T 428 2222,*
*www.brasserieharkema.nl*

**Gewoon Eten en Meer**

The name of this new 'lifestyle' deli in the up-and-coming Oost district is rather a mouthful, and appropriately means 'just food and more'. And it offers so much more. Acclaimed South African chef and founder Matthias Kleingeld has scoured the globe for high-quality condiments and uses mostly local ingredients in his top-notch takeaway dishes. The eclectic menu ranges from ravioli stuffed with pumpkin to couscous, salads, soups and home-made cakes. Bespoke gourmet picnics for four can be prepared with three days' notice.
*Beukenplein 18, T 665 5075, www.gewoonmeer.nl*

### Vuong

Despite its location near the touristy Leidseplein, restaurant/lounge Vuong oozes cool, thanks in part to its anonymous black facade. The interiors are a strict continuation of the noir colour scheme, as the furnishings, floor, walls and doors are all black. This dark experiment in monochrome minimalism works surprisingly well, as the orange oriental-style ceiling lights and table-top candles create a cosy ambience. The Asian-influenced menu offers more conservative palates dishes such as *moules et frites*, onion soup and oysters, and the upstairs lounge is popular for pre-clubbing cocktails.
*Korte Leidsedwarsstraat 51, T 580 5577, www.vuong.nl*

### De Kas

Five years ago, chef Gert Jan Hageman saved an old greenhouse on the edge of town and turned it into an acclaimed eaterie set literally in its own kitchen garden. The 1920s structure, which was modernised by designer Piet Boon, is bright and cheerful by day, tranquil and romantic by night.
*Kamerlingh Onneslaan 3, T 462 4562, www.restaurantdekas.nl*

#### Odeon

Since its days as one of the first concert halls in Amsterdam, Odeon has been a venue associated with controversy. The turn of the last century saw high-kicking cabaret acts taking centre stage, then it became a theatre, a cinema, an auction house and, in the 1950s, a notorious gay club that attracted the likes of Elton John, Freddie Mercury, Lou Reed and Jean Paul Gaultier. After a post-millennial facelift,

courtesy of Iding Design, its many spaces are once again pulling in the crowds. Odeon has two restaurants (the basement brasserie is open for lunch only), a small bar overlooking Singel, and a club that plays to a thirtysomething crowd. *Singel 460, T 521 8555, www.odeontheater.nl*

## Le Garage

The power-lunching media crowd that frequents Le Garage hasn't changed much since the 1980s, and neither have the mirrored interiors. Fortunately, the French regional food served here has kept its high standards too. If the dressy clientele and high prices aren't your style, pop next door to Le Garage's diffusion eaterie En Pluche (T 471 4695). *Ruysdaelstraat 54, T 679 7176*

### The Mansion

Despite the owners' best efforts, the crowd at this ambitious pleasuredome is more well-heeled preppie than cutting-edge cool, but The Mansion is still worth a visit for the fantastic cocktails alone. Guests are greeted by a huge black-and-white still of Marilyn Monroe and Frank Sinatra and are then funnelled into the warren of bars that makes up the entire ground floor. One is a ruched, pink, tented affair, another a cosy corner of mirrors and Perspex, while the main space boasts an impressive ceiling that pays homage to the Sistine Chapel. In the restaurant upstairs, Hong Kong chef Chan Lap Yan serves up fine modern Chinese cuisine. Downstairs, the basement Dim Sum Club is more casual.
*Hobbemastraat 2, T 616 6664, www.the-mansion.nl*

### Bar Arc

When the tourists flooding Bloemenmarkt have disappeared at the end of the day, the boisterous gay scene nearby comes to life. The bars here have long competed for this fickle crowd's pink euro with slick, gimmicky interiors. April, the oldest, has a revolving bar, so punters can cruise the room without moving. Yet the current favourite is Bar Arc, thanks to its long opening hours, the sophisticated lighting system, wenge wood interiors, inventive cocktail list and finger-food menu. Wednesday nights attract a mixed crowd dedicated to cut-price house drinks, such as a Remy Sour or Decadent Mojito, and Fridays are crammed from 5pm onwards. *Reguliersdwarsstraat 44, T 689 7070, www.bararc.com*

## Nomads

Nomads is Supperclub's (see p041) exotic Arabian cousin, and attracts groups of decadent revellers who prefer belly dancers to the stilt-walkers to be found at its more famous sibling. The interiors at Nomads are stunning, the staff sexy and attentive, although the place is often accused of being a style-over-substance affair – the food can be decidedly patchy. The long, meandering brass bar does serve excellent cocktails, though, and the Eastern-inspired sounds that increase in tempo as the evening progresses are guaranteed to get you on your feet. For an intimate evening, book one of the six small, private spaces in the Al' kubbah area, or for a more social experience reserve seats in the communal Wast ad-dar section, from where you can slip easily onto the mosaic dance floor.
*Rozengracht 133-1, T 344 6401, www.restaurantnomads.nl*

### Bar Bep

The 1970s-style Bar Bep may be small, but the food is both excellent and affordable. And its young, arty regulars make it a great spot for people-watching. In the summer, punters spill out onto the street, clutching their *vaasjes* (about half a pint of beer) and vodka lime sodas. To sample the city's louche side, cross the road to NL Lounge (T 622 7510), where flocked wallpaper and velvet drapes create the perfect habitat for Amsterdam's lounge lizards. In the winter, head for Finch (T 626 2461), one of the coolest contemporary brown cafés in town. The views of Prinsengracht canal from the terrace more than make up for the café's cramped conditions.
*Nieuwezijds Voorburgwal, T 626 5649*

### Club More

More's reputation as the city's premier dance space has faded drastically of late, as is so often the case in clubland. During the week, the club is often used as a venue for launches, fashion shows and corporate events, although at the weekend it can still pull off a good, glitzy club night. For a more casual option, head for local favourite Bitterzoet (T 521 3001), which plays jazz and hip hop downstairs and has a pool table and a smaller bar upstairs. Another late-night haunt is Sinners (T 620 1375), the current club of choice for the dressy, celebrity set, as it features wall-to-wall designer furniture and three dance floors. In order to get in, non-members must dazzle with their glad rags or show up before midnight.
*Rozengracht 133, T 344 6402,
www.clubmore.nl*

# INSIDER'S GUIDE
## DUNCAN STUTTERHEIM, ID&T FOUNDER

Since Duncan Stutterheim founded the entertainment and media group ID&T (www.id-t.com), which specialises in hosting mammoth dance events, more than a decade ago, it has spiralled into an international enterprise that currently has shares in Slam! FM radio station and four hospitality venues. When he's not exporting the strobes and sounds of big-name DJs to Belgium, Germany, Spain, Poland and Russia, Stutterheim savours his spare time in his home town Amsterdam.

The French-Vietnamese café Vuong (see p049) is Stutterheim's favourite eaterie for breakfast, and for lunch he heads to Spring (Willemsparkweg 177, T 675 4421, www.restaurantspring.nl), one of Concrete's deeply fashionable creations. For dinner, he'll book a table at Cinema Paradiso (Westerstraat 184-186, T 623 7344) or Dynasty (Reguliersdwarsstraat 30, T 626 8400), which has an Asian-style menu. In the evening, Stutterheim likes to relax with a beer in one of the traditional bars in the Jordaan, or share a joint with friends at Café Coffeeshop Rokerij (Lange Leidsedwarsstraat 41, T 626 3060, www.rokerij.net). If he feels like dressing up and having a glamorous night out, he'll head for The Mansion (see p056), which he believes serves the best cocktails in town. As megaclubs are Stutterheim's day job, the dance venue he likes best is the tiny Studio 80 (Rembrandtplein 17, T 521 8333, www.studio-80.nl).

# ARCHITOUR

## A GUIDE TO AMSTERDAM'S ICONIC BUILDINGS

Dutch architecture is some of the most innovative and exciting in Europe right now. Unfortunately, Amsterdam is not really at its forefront. The truth is, of course, that the city has managed very nicely, thank you, with its appealing and justly celebrated canalside vernacular – all gables, large windows and lifting beams, accessorised by suitably well-regimented lines of shade-giving trees. After showing brief modernist tendencies at the beginning of the 20th century – with the first flowering of the Amsterdam School and its acknowledged master Hendrik Petrus Berlage – the city largely lost the will to innovate and decided instead to stick with what it had, architecturally speaking, that is. It promptly curled up and slept for most of the next hundred years.

When KNSM, the last of the city's shipping giants, tanked in 1977, Havens Oost, the eastern docklands area, was earmarked for radical reinvention. Four peninsulas were added to the River Ij and a whole new neighbourhood was dreamed up. Unlike most dreary docklands schemes, though, this one was aimed at aesthetes not at bankers, and involved the participation of almost every architect in town – around 60 of them at the final count. The result is a modern interpretation of classic tract housing, one of the buzziest neighbourhoods in Benelux, and, if nothing else, a welcome change of pace from Amsterdam's familiar canalside properties. *For all addresses, see Resources.*

**Living Tomorrow Pavilion**

Architects Ben van Berkel and Caroline Bos are as well known for their theoretical work as for their innovative practice, UN Studio. They don't always take on the most glamorous projects (theirs is undoubtedly the world's most beautiful waste disposal facility in Delft), but they are always interesting. The Living Tomorrow Pavilion in Amsterdam Zuidoost marries the theoretical and practical sides of their work, offering visitors a glimpse of the living concepts and technologies of the future, some of which are available today. It's a future that the set designers of films such as *2001: A Space Odyssey* would surely have approved – all clean, curvilinear shapes. *De Entrée 300, Amsterdam Zuidoost, T 203 0400, www.livtom.com, www.unstudio.com*

**Hope, Love and Fortune**
Even if the architectural delights of
Borneo Sporenburg are starting to pall,
and you can't inveigle an invite into one
of the flats, you must see the facade
of this office and apartment complex,
designed by Rudy Uytenhaak in 2002,
before heading back to town. Made of
Norwegian marble, it was produced with
the artist Willem Oorebeek.
*Rietlandenterras 2-54, Borneo
Sporenburg*

### ARCAM

Built in 1986, and still looking like a vision of some alternate future, the Amsterdam Centre for Architecture, set up in the heart of the city, should be the first stop in any architour of Amsterdam. Intended as a public information point for new and old buildings, it hosts provocative talks, exhibitions and lectures. A particularly good feature of the centre's recommended tours are the archishuttle guides to points of interest on major tram and bus routes, which enable the visitor to see the sights without being herded in a dreadful tourist group. ARCAM's airy waterside HQ, which was designed by René van Zuuk, also makes a good meeting point.
*Prins Hendrikkade 600, T 620 4878, www.arcam.nl*

### Borneo Sporenburg Bridges

At the height of its construction frenzy at the tail end of the 1990s, almost 60 architects were involved in the creation of the new neighbourhood of Borneo Sporenburg. Fortunately, the results were much less jarring than this melange of creators might have suggested. One of the keys to the overall success of the development were the three bridges that connect the different areas and provide a unifying architectural feature. The work of architects West 8, the bridges have become destinations in their own right. The tallest one, designed to let boats sail into the marina, provides a vantage point for viewing the whole neighbourhood and, dare we say it, spying on the cute locals enjoying their sun terraces.

*Stuurmankade-Panamakade, Borneo Sporenburg, www.west8.nl*

### Silodam

Architects MVRDV hail from Rotterdam,
the largest container port in Europe, so
it was perhaps no surprise when they
referenced shipping containers in this
apartment building on the Amsterdam
dockside. There is an amazing variety in
terms of height, depth and the number
of floors among the 157 flats, some of
which are available for short lets.
*Oude Houthaven, www.silodam.org,
www.mvrdv.nl*

# SHOPPING

## THE CITY'S BEST SHOPS AND WHAT TO BUY

With its myriad shops and boutiques – around 10,000 at the last count – any visitor to Amsterdam with a sharp eye is guaranteed to return home laden with loot. The most popular shopping district is undoubtedly the Negen Straatjes (Nine Streets) straddling the four principal canals, where old curiosity shops stand cheek by jowl with novelty boutiques specialising in anything from candles (Kramer, Reestraat 20, T 626 5274) to toothbrushes (De Witte Tandenwinkel, Runstraat 5, T 623 3443). Nearby Rozengracht is almost entirely dedicated to interiors stores, from the gleaming Wonen 2000 (Rozengracht 215-223, T 521 8112) to the retro-fabulous treasure trove that is SPRMRKT (see p080). Design junkies should head straight for the two legendary creative centres – Frozen Fountain (see p084) and Droog (opposite), whose tiny showroom displays a collection of products, from the deeply cool to the downright kooky.

Old-school Amsterdammers shop on Cornelis Schuytstraat and dismiss PC Hooftstraat, with its string of branded boutiques, as the stomping ground of the nouveau riche and the mafiosi. Students and artists furnish their apartments and fill their wardrobes in the gritty but groovy area of De Pijp, while cavernous outlets such as Pol's Potten (see p076) and Keet in Huis (see p086) in the slick eastern docklands cater to young yuppy families. *For all addresses, see Resources.*

**Droog**

In 1993, designer Gijs Bakker and design critic and historian Renny Ramakers joined forces to form what was to become the country's premier creative platform, Droog. Droog means 'dry', and references the quick wit, unadorned informality and irony for which both the Dutch and the products of this non-profit foundation are famed. Bubble wrap-inspired glasses, plasticized water droplets which turn a clear bathroom window opaque, and a set of drawers tied together to form a chest (above), designed by Tejo Remy, are some of the pieces sold at Droog's beautiful headquarters. Many of the products on sale are limited editions.
*Staalstraat 7a-7b, T 523 5050, www.droogdesign.nl*

**Tommyz Toko**
Tommy Hagen is no ordinary hairstylist. His passion for interiors, fashion, music, graphic design and street art inspired him to join forces with vintage furniture dealer Edwin de Koeyer, and launch this alternative salon. Since its opening two years ago, the salon has become a creative hub within De Pijp.
*Daniel Stalpertstraat 97, T 638 7872, www.tommyztoko.nl*

## Pol's Potten

Since he started selling pots from Spain and Portugal in a small shop in Jordaan 20 years ago, Eric Pol's name has become synonymous with interiors. His huge emporium in the eastern docklands has shelves stacked with ceramics, such as the delftware-inspired bowls and egg cups, €13 each (above), by Anne-Marie Jetten, candles, glassware, fabrics, lamps and toys. Many products, such as the 'Twiggy' candleholder, €159, and flocked 'Delight' lampshade, €195 (both above), have been designed in-house. In the furniture section, you'll find antiques imported from Asia, as well as modern pieces by Dutch designers. Customers who yearn for the distinctive Pol's Potten look at home can book a free interiors consultation. *KNSMlaan 39, T 419 3541, www.polspotten.nl*

DE
OORSPRONKELIJKE

KOFFIE

DE ENIGE ECHTE RADEMAKER HAAGSCHE HOPJES

*Rademaker*®

HOPJES

HOLLAND

ALLEEN ECHT MET
DIT MERK

**Dutch Delicacies**

If you've ever tasted aged or cumin Gouda from legendary deli De Kaaskamer, you'll have realised why the Dutch export the younger version of this famous cheese and its plasticky red cousin Edam, and keep the best stuff for themselves. To stock up on other Dutch gastronomic treats, stop at any Albert Hein supermarket and fill your basket with the following: Bols *genever* (Dutch gin); *stroopwafels* (honey waffles), Droste (chocolate pastilles), Hopjes (coffee-flavoured drops; above); Muisjes (sugared aniseed sprinkles) by De Ruyter, which are traditionally eaten at baby showers, and, lastly, Indonesian sambal (chilli sauce) by Koningsvogel.
*De Kaaskamer, Runstraat 7, T 623 3483*

**Lairesse Apotheek**
The back-lit periodic table that arcs
around the facade of the Lairesse chemist
near Jacob Obrechtstraat gives an initial
indication of the state-of-the-art interiors
in this futuristic pharmacy. Architects
Concrete designed glowing green medicine
cabinets, containing both herbal and
conventional cures for every affliction
imaginable. It also created a glass reading
room at the back, where terminals give
free access to a medical database of
information on symptoms of various
illnesses and alternative therapies. A
perspex cube has been designated as
the deposit box for the safe disposal
of unwanted drugs (a standard feature
in Dutch chemists across the land for
many years). Situated in Oud Zuid,
Lairesse is worth a visit after a tour of
the major museums.
*De Lairessestraat 40, T 662 1022,*
*www.delairesseapotheek.nl*

## SPRMRKT

For years Bebob Design (T 624 5763) was Amsterdam's principal peddler of retro furniture, but its location (a long schlep from the city centre) and high prices have made it a definite second to the deeply fashionable SPRMRKT, which opened a few years ago. This store's entrance is hung with groovy retro light fittings and the occasional piece of tasteful taxidermy, while the cavernous hall is clustered with classic 1950s furniture, new work by young designers, such as Mark Meerdink's screen, €1,650 (above), and racks of hip clothes, including vintage 1970s shirts in their original packaging. Be sure to check out the catalogue, showing pieces stored off site, and the retro Belgian wallpaper at the back of the shop.

*Rozengracht 191-193, T 330 5601,*
*www.sprmrkt.nl*

### Negen Straatjes

If you're looking for novelty keepsakes that are likely to appreciate in value, scour the Negen Straatjes south of Raadhuisstraat. With a little searching, you may come across some surprising gems, from breakfast sets showing city scenes, €5-€20 per piece, and Cor Unum ceramics, from €25, to porcelain delftware houses filled with Bols *genever*, from €15 each (all above), which KLM has been presenting to its first-class passengers since 1952. Nic Nic (T 622 8523) is a good place to start your quest. For retro lighting, head for Fifties Sixties (T 623 2653), and to pick up more original purchases, visit Boekie Woekie (T 639 0507), which sells one-off books hand-made by artists.

### Shoebaloo

Since opening a humble shoe shop in the Jordaan in 1976, Hartog A Streim has grown into the country's premier trader in posh footwear. For his most spectacular outlet on PC Hooftstraat, he commissioned architects Meyer en Van Schooten to create a futuristic *Battlestar Galactica* experience. The pod seating and ambient lighting have proved so successful in shifting the store's huge stock of unisex shoes (Dolce & Gabbana, Prada, Marc Jacobs, Viktor & Rolf and Streim's own men's line Arturo) that Streim has opened another shop (decked out in black leather clad with floral motifs) selling accessories on nearby Cornelis Shuytstraat.
*PC Hooftstraat 80, T 671 2210,
www.shoebaloo.nl*

**Frozen Fountain**

Although Frozen Fountain's two floors of gallery space showcases well-known brands such as Driade, Flos and Edra, it is principally a creative hothouse for home-grown talent. Piet Hein Eek and Marcel Wanders launched their careers here, so Frozen Fountain is hallowed ground for aspiring Dutch designers. Local crafts are often reinterpreted with a quirky contemporary twist – check out the collections by Hella Jongerius and Studio Job, which was commissioned by the country's oldest ceramics house, Royal Tichelaar Makkum. Less pricey, but just as beautiful, are the plates (above) and dishes, from €19, by Tord Boontje. *Prinsengracht 645, T 622 9375, www.frozenfountain.nl*

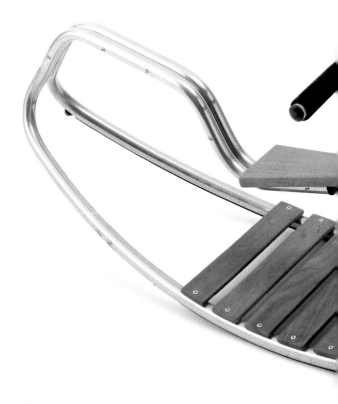

### Keet in Huis

It's not easy to come up with gifts even for the baby, toddler, nephew or niece. For one thing, they already seem to have every designer accessory ever created. One solution might be to head for Keet in Huis, which stocks ergonomic potties, bespoke cots, kiddie clothes, hand-made toys and the chunky, funky Bugaboo prams. Even the classic rocking horse, €195 (above), has undergone a redesign,

courtesy of Chris Slutter. Then pop across to 90 Square Metres (T 419 2525), where you will find organic cosmetics, Japanese T-shirts, Finnish fashion, rare trainers and edgy art books and magazines – perfect gifts for the big kid in all of us.
*KNSMlaan 297, T 419 5958,*
*www.keetinhuis.nl*

# SPORTS AND SPAS
## WORK OUT, CHILL OUT OR JUST WATCH

When it snows in Amsterdam, the city takes on a magical, picture-book allure, though while tourists admire its muffled, winter-wonderland beauty, locals are busy checking the temperature to see if it will drop low enough for long enough to don their skates. Some of the canals, principally the Keizersgracht, become glittering highways teeming with enthusiasts practising their speed-skating, in case the big freeze reaches Friesland and the famous Eleven Cities Race is declared. Due to global warming, the last one took place a decade ago, so Amsterdammers have to make do with zooming around the Jaap Edenbaan rink (Radioweg 64, T 694 9894), where skates can be hired from November to February. This national sporting obsession continues into the summer, when every Friday 3,000 in-line skaters take to the streets for a 15-20km race around town (www.fridaynightskate.com).

Cycling is so much a part of Dutch culture that bicycles have right of way in Holland; always keep an ear out for them – they are not known as 'the whispering death' for nothing. You can hire bicycles at MacBike (Weteringschans 2, T 620 0985). Mirandalaan (De Mirandalaan 9, T 546 4444), which has both indoor and outdoor pools, a wave machine and a pebble 'beach', has recently been usurped as the city's premier swimming venue by the slick, centrally located Het Marnix (Marnixplein, T 530 6872).
*For all addresses, see Resources.*

### Klimhal

Clambering up one of this climbing centre's five fibreglass walls, which are studded with multicoloured holds offering different routes and levels of difficulty, is one of the most popular pastimes for sporty, thrill-seeking Amsterdammers. The Lead Climbing Wall is 21m high, and is often used for national and international competitions. The other, less vertiginous options include Boulderhall, which is carpeted with crash mats, and the Ship, both of which have a 4m maximum climb. Outside opening hours (10.30am-5pm), there are regular two-hour courses on offer for beginners, but experienced climbers, who don't need any instruction, can access the main wall at earlier times, as long as they call ahead.
*Naritaweg 48, T 681 0121,*
*www.klimhalamsterdam.nl*

**Medico Vision**
Housed in the former Olympic stadium,
Medico Vision offers a day pass, €15,
which allows guests access to 1,500
sq m of space and top-of-the-range
fitness and cardio equipment. The sleek
Gym 80 machines even manage to look
good and inviting at the same time. A
sauna, steam bath, running track and
lounge complete the fitness picture.
*Olympisch Stadion 23, T 675 2313,*
*www.medicovision.nl*

### Squash City

As its name suggests, this centre's 13 glass-backed squash courts are the main attraction. A day pass here costs under €10, though the 45-minute match slots should be booked at least a week in advance; private 25-minute lessons with a professional coach for €26 are also available. Other wellbeing facilities on offer include a gym, an aerobics area with yoga, step and spinning classes, an in-house physiotherapist, and a lavish spa, with two saunas, a solarium, Turkish steam bath and a large relaxation lounge (above). Following a recent facelift, the centre now has a restaurant and a bar.
*Ketelmakerstraat 6, T 626 7883,*
*www.squashcity.nl*

## Soap Company

If you need to scrub up or wind down during your stay in Amsterdam, set aside an hour for a facial or a massage at the Soap Company (above), where treatments cost €20-€700. A more decadent option is Sauna Deco (T 623 8215), where you can admire the chic art deco interior, salvaged from a Parisian department store, while being pummelled Swedish-style into a state of dazed relaxation. Koan Float (T 555 0333) offers all of the above and more; its main treatment consists of an ethereal half-hour spent floating in a saline solution, inside a contraption that resembles a hollowed-out Reliant Robin. This is quite an extraordinary experience, as long as you (and the person before you) remembered to pee beforehand.
*Spuistraat 281, T 428 9660,*
*www.soapcompany.com*

**Arena Stadium**
Amsterdam is so obsessed with its
world-famous football team that, in
the monumental Arena stadium, there
is a museum, World of Ajax, dedicated
to its star players and trophies. Since
the stadium opened in 1996, a million
die-hard fans have queued up for the
behind-the-scenes tour.
*Arena Boulevard 1, T 311 1336,*
*www.amsterdamarena.nl*

# ESCAPES

## WHERE TO GO IF YOU WANT TO LEAVE TOWN

As the Netherlands is such a tiny country (you can drive across it in two hours), a day trip from Amsterdam throws up almost innumerable options. Art fans should head for The Hague, which is only a 45-minute train ride from Centraal Station. Here, the striking yellow-brick Gemeente Museum (Stadhouderslaan 41, T 70 338 1111, www.gemeentemuseum.nl), built by the legendary Dutch architect Hendrick Petrus Berlage, has an impressive permanent collection, including canvases by Mondrian, Monet and Picasso. The Mauritshuis (Korte Vijverberg 8, T 70 302 3456, www.mauritshuis.nl) shows Dutch Golden Age masterpieces, notably Vermeer's *Girl with a Pearl Earring* and *View of Delft*, a haunting portrayal of the artist's home town, which is a 20-minute tram ride from the centre of town.

Historic Haarlem is practically a suburb of Amsterdam (it's only 15 minutes by train from Centraal Station), but has a well-heeled, provincial vibe, the famous Frans Hals Museum (Groot Heiligland 62, T 23 511 5775, www.franshalsmuseum.nl) and Ibiza-style beach clubs in nearby Bloemendaal. Rotterdam's cityscape is a hymn to the Dutch love of innovative contemporary architecture, while Hortus Botanicus (www.hortusleiden.nl) in the picturesque town of Leiden (the birthplace of Rembrandt) is an ode to the country's obsession with plants and flowers.

*For all addresses, see Resources.*

### The Weekend Company

If a day trip within Holland won't provide enough of a cultural contrast to your Amsterdam experience, consider spending a night or two further afield. Maastricht, which is a mere two and a half hours away by train (from Centraal Station), has a far more Western European flavour, as it is wedged between Belgium, Germany and Luxembourg. Antwerp, Brussels and Paris are alternative destinations, all easily accessible by train or plane. The Weekend Company (above), next to Amsterdam's famous flower market, offers attractive deals for stays at five-star hotels in all these cities.
*Singel 540, T 419 1218,*
*www.weekendcompany.nl*

**Dick Bruna House**

The name of the graphic artist Dick Bruna may not be instantly recognisable, but his most famous creation, Miffy, the cute, cross-mouthed white rabbit, most certainly is. Since the first book of Miffy's adventures was published in 1955, Bruna has become a design icon and an international publishing phenomenon; book sales topping 85 million worldwide have made Bruna Holland's most successful living artist. Utrecht's Centraal Museum (www.centraalmuseum.nl) has recently opened Dick Bruna House, a museum dedicated to all of Bruna's oeuvre, including 2,000 of his graphic book covers and more than 100 posters, postcards and prints. Also on show are original sketches, and pencil and ink drawings illustrating the development of the Miffy character.

*Agnietenstraat 2, Utrecht, T 30 236 2392, www.dickbrunahuis.com*

### Kröller-Müller Museum

The enormous Hoge Veluwe National Park (www.hogeveluwe.nl), which spans 5,500 hectares, was left to the Dutch state by a phenomenally wealthy, philanthropic Dutch-German couple, Helene and Anton Kröller-Müller. Anton bought the estate as a hunting ground, while Helene used it to house her incredible collection of canvases by Léger, Mondrian, Picasso, Renoir, Seurat and Van Gogh, now in the museum. Take a turn round the Rietveld Pavilion, which is surrounded by Barbara Hepworth sculptures, and the surreal installation by Jean Dubuffet, then jump on one of the free bicycles provided to zoom across the network of perfectly maintained cycle paths, arriving at the couple's exquisite hunting lodge.
*Houtkampweg 6, Otterio, T 31 859 1241, www.kmm.nl*

### Bloemendaal

Since being acknowledged as the coolest stretch of coast in the country, Bloemendaal has become a hot destination for Amsterdammers in search of sun, sand and the latest sounds. Beat the crowds and take an early train to Haarlem, then a bus or a taxi to the sea. From spring until late September, the beachfront becomes one massive lounge club-cum-alfresco nightclub. Head for Republiek Beach Club, or for a hippyish hangout walk a bit further down the beach, to Woodstock 69. If you're too cool for this scene, head north up the coast to join the smaller, even trendier beach community at Wijk aan Zee. *Zeeweg 1, Bloemendaal, www.republiek.tv*

### Keukenhof

With seven million bulbs blooming at once in 3 sq km of parkland, a day trip to Keukenhof (45 minutes by train from Centraal Station) is a must for tulip addicts and floral fetishists. Four pavilions house exhibitions offering top tips for the green-fingered. The bulbs are planted in layers, so as one layer dies, another grows from underneath to replace it, which guarantees a permanent floral carpet of colour from March until May. If you miss this spring spectacle, you can still stock up on bulbs for your own garden at Amsterdam's Bloemenmarkt. For six months of blooms, buy snowdrops to flower in February, striped squills for March, tulips for April, fritillaries for May, and alliums for June and July. *Stationsweg 166a, Lisse, T 25 246 5555, www.keukenhof.nl*

### Rotterdam

Head for Holland's most vibrant city and explore the bold and experimental 20th-century architecture that has given the city one of Europe's most daring skylines. Rotterdam has designated 2007 its Year of Architecture, but until then you can take an Archiguide tour (T 10 205 1519) of its most famous buildings and burgeoning design district by bus, bike or on foot. Next take a turn round the Netherlands Architecture Institute (T 10 440 1200) and the next-door Sonneveld House, which was designed by Brinkman and Van der Vlugt, before jumping in a taxi to the iconic Cube Houses (above). *Overblaak 70, T 10 414 2285, www.kubuswoning.nl*

# NOTES

**SKETCHES AND MEMOS**

# RESOURCES
## ADDRESSES AND ROOM RATES

### LANDMARKS

**010 The Whale**
*Baron GA Tindalplein*
*Borneo Sporenburg*
*www.cie.nl*

**012 NEMO**
*Oosterdok 2*
*T 531 3233*
*www.e-nemo.nl*

**013 Anne Frank House**
*Prinsengracht 267*
*T 556 7105*
*www.annefrank.org*

**014 Van Gogh Museum**
*Paulus Potterstraat 7*
*T 570 5200*
*www.vangoghmuseum.nl*

### HOTELS

**016 Amsterdam American**
Room rates:
double, €310;
suite, €385
*Leidsekade 97*
*T 556 3000*
*www.amsterdamam erican.com*

**016 Canal House Hotel**
Room rates:
double, €140-€190
*Keizersgracht 148*
*T 622 5182*
*www.canalhousehotel.com*

**016 Marcel's Creative Exchange**
Room rates:
double, €90-€120
*Leidsestraat 87*
*T 622 9834*
*www.marcelamsterdam.nl*

**016 Hotel V**
Room rates:
double, €140
*Victorieplein 42*
*T 662 3233*
*www.hotelv.nl*

**016 Kien**
Room rates:
double, €125
*Tweede Weteringdwarsstraat 65*
*T 428 5262*
*www.marykien.nl*

**016 The Grand**
Room rates:
double, €440;
suite, €520
*Oudezijds Voorburgwal 197*
*T 555 3111*
*www.thegrand.nl*

**017 Lloyd Hotel**
Room rates:
double, €80-€95;
deluxe room, €120-€145;
superior room, €270-€295
*Oosterlijke Handelskade 34*
*T 561 3636*
*www.lloydhotel.com*

**018 The College Hotel**
Room rates:
double, €235;
deluxe room, €285;
junior suite, €470
*Roelof Hartstraat 1*
*T 571 1511*
*www.thecollegehotel.com*

**020 Hotel Seven One Seven**
Room rates:
double, €405;
suite, €460;
deluxe suite, €660
*Prinsengracht 717*
*T 427 0717*
*www.717hotel.nl*

**021 Lute Suites**
Room rates:
suites, €275-€345
*Amsteldijk Zuid 54-58*
*Ouderkerk aan den Amstel*
*T 472 2462*
*www.lutesuites.com*

**024 InterContinental Amstel**
Room rates:
double, €390-€575;
suite, €540-€725;
deluxe, €780-€1,275
*Professor Tulpplein 1*
*T 622 6060*
*www.ichotelsgroup.com*

**025 't Hotel**
Room rates:
double, €145-€165
*Leliegracht 18*
*T 422 2741*
*www.thotel.nl*
**028 The Dylan**
Room rates:
double, €420;
suite, €720;
deluxe suite, €1,590
*Keizersgracht 384*
*T 530 2010*
*www.dylanamsterdam.com*
**030 Hotel Arena**
Room rates:
double, €80-€110;
suite, €225-€275
*'s-Gravesandestraat 51*
*T 694 7444*
*www.hotelarena.nl*

## 24 HOURS
**032 FOAM**
**Photography Museum**
*Keizersgracht 609*
*T 551 6500*
*www.foam.nl*
**032 Nieuwe Kerk**
*Dam Square*
*T 638 6909*
*www.nieuwekerk.nl*
**032 Rembrandt House**
*Jodenbreestraat 4*
*T 520 0400*
*www.rembrandthuis.nl*

**032 Rijksmuseum**
*Stadhouderskade 42*
*T 674 7000*
*www.rijksmuseum.nl*
**033 Barney's**
*Haarlemmerstraat 98*
*T 625 9761*
*www.barneys.biz*
**033 11**
*Oosterdokkade 35*
*T 625 5999*
*www.ilove11.nl*
**033 Stedelijk Museum**
*2nd-3rd floor, Post CS*
*Building*
*Oosterdokskade 5*
*T 573 2911*
*www.stedelijk.nl*
**034 Amstelkring**
**Museum**
*Oudezijds Voorburgwal 40*
*T 624 6604*
*www.museumamstel*
*kring.nl*
**035 Amsterdam**
**Historical Museum**
*Kalverstraat 92*
*T 523 1822*
*www.ahm.nl*
**035 Begijnhof**
*Gedempte Begijnensloot,*
*Begijnhof 30*
*T 622 1918*
*www.begijnhof*
*amsterdam.nl*
**036 Van Gogh Museum**
*Paulus Potterstraat 7*
*T 570 5200*
*www.vangoghmuseum.nl*

**038 18twintig**
*Ferdinand Bolstraat 18-20*
*T 470 0651*
*www.18twintig.nl*
**038 Werck**
*Prinsengracht 277*
*T 627 4079*
*www.werck.nl*

## URBAN LIFE
**040 Café De Jaren**
*Nieuwe Doelenstraat 20-22*
*T 625 5771*
**040 D'Vijff Vlieghen**
*Spuistraat 294-302*
*T 530 4060*
**040 Het Blauwe**
**Theehuis**
*Vondelpark 5*
*T 662 0254*
**040 Lunchcafé**
**Singel 404**
*Singel 404*
*T 428 0154*
**040 Morlangs**
*Keizersgracht 449*
*T 625 2681*
*www.morlang.nl*
**040 Odessa**
*Veemkade 259*
*T 419 3010*
*www.de-odessa.nl*
**040 Walem**
*Keizersgracht 449*
*T 625 3544*

**041 Supperclub**
*Jonge Roelensteeg 21*
*T 344 6400*
*www.supperclub.nl*
**044 Onassis**
*Westerdoksdijk 40*
*T 330 0456*
*www.onassisamsterdam.nl*
**045 Envy**
*Prinsengracht 381*
*T 344 6407*
*www.envy.nl*
**046 Brasserie Harkema**
*Nes 67*
*T 428 2222*
*www.brasserieharkema.nl*
**048 Gewoon Eten**
**en Meer**
*Beukenplein 18*
*T 665 5075*
*www.gewoonmeer.nl*
**049 Vuong**
*Korte Leidsedwarsstraat 51*
*T 580 5577*
*www.vuong.nl*
**050 De Kas**
*Kamerlingh Onneslaan 3*
*T 462 4562*
*www.restaurantdekas.nl*
**052 Odeon**
*Singel 460*
*T 521 8555*
*www.odeontheater.nl*
**054 En Pluche**
*Ruysdaelstraat 48*
*T 471 4695*
*www.enpluche.nl*

**054 Le Garage**
*Ruysdaelstraat 54*
*T 679 7176*
*www.restaurantlegarage.nl*
**056 The Mansion**
*Hobbemastraat 2*
*T 616 6664*
*www.the-mansion.nl*
**057 Bar Arc**
*Reguliersdwarsstraat 44*
*T 689 7070*
*www.bararc.com*
**058 Nomads**
*Rozengracht 133-1*
*T 344 6401*
*www.restaurantnomads.nl*
**060 Bar Bep**
*Nieuwezijds*
*Voorburgwal 260*
*T 626 5649*
**060 Finch**
*Noordermarkt 5*
*T 626 2461*
**060 NL Lounge**
*Nieuwezijds*
*Voorburgwal 169*
*T 622 7510*
**061 Bitterzoet**
*Spuistraat 2*
*T 521 3001*
*www.bitterzoet.com*
**061 Club More**
*Rozengracht 133*
*T 344 6402*
*www.clubmore.nl*
**061 Sinners**
*Wagenstraat 3-7*
*T 620 1375*
*www.sinners.nl*

**062 Café Coffeeshop**
**Rokerij**
*Lange Leidsedwarsstraat 41*
*T 626 3060*
*www.rokerij.net*
**062 Cinema Paradiso**
*Westerstraat 184-186*
*T 623 7344*
**062 Dynasty**
*Reguliersdwarsstraat 30*
*T 626 8400*
**062 Spring**
*Willemsparkweg 177*
*T 675 4421*
*www.restaurantspring.nl*
**062 Studio 80**
*Rembrandtplein 17*
*T 521 8333*
*www.studio-80.nl*

**ARCHITOUR**
**065 Living**
**Tomorrow Pavilion**
*De Entrée 300*
*Amsterdam Zuidoost*
*T 203 0400*
*www.livtom.com*
*www.unstudio.com*
**066 Hope, Love**
**and Fortune**
*Rietlandenterras 2-54*
*Borneo Sporenburg*
**068 ARCAM**
*Prins Hendrikkade 600*
*T 620 4878*
*www.arcam.nl*

**093 Koan Float**
*Herengracht 321*
*T 555 0333*
*www.koanfloat.nl*
**093 Sauna Deco**
*Herengracht 115*
*T 623 8215*
*www.saunadeco.nl*
**093 Soap Company**
*Spuistraat 281*
*T 428 9660*
*www.soapcompany.com*
**094 Amsterdam Football Arena**
*Arena Boulevard 1*
*Amsterdam Zuidoost*
*T 311 1336*
*www.amsterdamarena.nl*

## ESCAPES
**096 Frans Hals Museum**
*Groot Heiligland 62*
*Haarlem*
*T 23 511 5775*
*www.franshalsmuseum.nl*
**096 Gemeente Museum**
*Stadhouderslaan 41*
*Den Haag*
*T 70 338 1111*
*www.gemeentemuseum.nl*
**096 Hortus Botanicus**
*Rapenburg 73*
*Leiden*
*T 71 527 7249*
*www.hortusleiden.nl*

**096 The Mauritshuis**
*Korte Vijverberg 8*
*Den Haag*
*T 70 302 3456*
*www.mauritshuis.nl*
**097 The Weekend Company**
*Singel 540*
*T 419 1218*
*www.weekendcompany.nl*
**098 Dick Bruna House**
*Agnietenstraat 2*
*Utrecht*
*T 30 236 2392*
*www.dickbrunahuis.com*
**100 Kröller-Müller Museum**
*Houtkampweg 6*
*Otterlo*
*T 31 859 1241*
*www.kmm.nl*
**100 Hoge Veluwe National Park**
*www.hogeveluwe.nl*
**101 Republiek**
*Zeeweg 1*
*Bloemendaal*
*www.republiek.tv*
**102 Keukenhof**
*Stationsweg 166a*
*Lisse*
*T 25 246 5555*
*www.keukenhof.nl*
**103 Cube Houses**
*Overblaak 70*
*Rotterdam*
*T 10 414 2285*
*www.kubuswoning.nl*

**103 Netherlands Architecture Institute**
*Museumpark 25*
*Rotterdam*
*T 10 440 1200*
*www.nai.nl*
**103 Rotterdam Archiguides**
*Beursplein 37*
*Rotterdam*
*T 10 205 1519*
*www.rotterdam-archiguides.nl*

## WALLPAPER* CITY GUIDES

**Editorial Director**
Richard Cook

**Art Director**
Loran Stosskopf
**Series Editor**
Jeroen Bergmans
**Project Editor**
Rachael Moloney
**Series Retail Editor**
Emma Moore
**Executive**
**Managing Editor**
Jessica Firmin

**Chief Designer**
Ben Blossom
**Designers**
Dominic Bell
Sara Martin
Ingvild Sandal
**Map Illustrator**
Russell Bell

**Photography Editor**
Emma Blau
**Photography Assistant**
Jasmine Labeau

**Sub-Editor**
Paul Sentobe
**Editorial Assistant**
Milly Nolan

**Wallpaper* Group**
**Editor-in-Chief**
Jeremy Langmead
**Creative Director**
Tony Chambers
**Publishing Director**
Fiona Dent

**Thanks to**
Paul Barnes
Meirion Pritchard

## PHAIDON

**Phaidon Press Limited**
Regent's Wharf
All Saints Street
London N1 9PA

**Phaidon Press Inc**
180 Varick Street
New York, NY 10014

www.phaidon.com

First published 2006
© 2006 Phaidon Press
Limited

ISBN 0 7148 4681 3

A CIP Catalogue record for
this book is available from
the British Library.

All prices are correct at
time of going to press, but
are subject to change.

Printed in China

## PHOTOGRAPHERS

**Amsterdam Tourism & Convention Board**
Amsterdam, City View, inside front cover

**Marcel Christ**
'Delight' lampshade;
'Twiggy' candleholder;
Anne-Marie Jetten
ceramics, p076
Hopjes, p077
Mark Meerdink screen,
p080
Breakfast set; KLM houses;
Cor Unum ceramics, p081
Tord Boontje plate, p085
Rocking horse, p086

**Michel Claus**
Le Garage, pp054-055

**Concrete Architectural Associates**
Supperclub, p041
Nomads, p058-059
Bar Bep, p060
Club More, p061
The Weekend Company,
p097

**Reineke Ekering**
Soap Company, p093

**Bob Goedewagen**
Tejo Remy chest, p073

**Pascal van Houtert**
Frozen Fountain, p084

**Luue Kramer**
Van Gogh Museum, p037

**Kim van der Leden**
Envy, p045

**Jeroen Musch**
Brasserie Harkema,
pp046-047
The Mansion, p056
Lairesse Apotheek,
pp078-079
Shoebaloo, pp082-083

**Ferry Andre de la Porte**
Dick Bruna House,
pp098-099

**Misha de Ridder**
The Whale, pp010-011
NEMO, p012
Anne Frank House, p013
Van Gogh Museum,
pp014-015
Lloyd Hotel, p017
Hotel Seven One Seven,
p020
Lute Suites, p021
Amstelkring Museum,
p034

Amsterdam Historical
Museum, p035
Van Gogh Museum, p036
Gewoon Eten en Meer, p048
De Kas, pp050-051
Duncan Stutterheim, p063
Living Tomorrow Pavilion,
p065
Hope, Love and Fortune,
pp066-067
Borneo Sporenburg
Bridge, p069
Silodam, pp070-071
Tommyz Toko, pp074-075
Klimhal, p089
Kröller-Müller Museum,
p100
Bloemendaal, p101
Cube Houses, p103

**Louis van de Vuurst**
Arena Stadium, pp094-095

**Wim Ruigrok**
ARCAM, p068

**Wouter**
Bar Arc, p057

**Illustration
Karine Faou**
Keukenhof, p102

# AMSTERDAM
## A COLOUR-CODED GUIDE TO THE CITY'S HOT 'HOODS

**DE PIJP**
The most multicultural district, not just in Amsterdam, but in the whole of Europe

**WESTERPARK**
 A poster child for the redemptive power of good architecture. Catch it on the way up

**CENTRUM**
Increasingly the preserve of sin, sleaze and stag parties, but still fun around the fringes

**JORDAAN**
If this were any more perfect (all cool cafés and delicious denizens), it would be at Epcot

**HAVENS OOST**
Home to the one grandiose docklands regeneration scheme that actually seems to work

**OUD ZUID**
More than just a museum quarter, the city's first suburb is staging a chic comeback

For a full description of each neighbourhood,
including the places you really must not miss, see the Introduction